Read for Meaning

Sequence

You will need

• Leveled Readers   • paper   • pencil

15 min.

● Choose and read a book provided by your teacher. Think about the order of events in the story. List three important events from the book in the correct order. Use signal words to show the sequence.

▲ Choose and read a book provided by your teacher. Think about the order of events. Write three sentences that tell the sequence. Use signal words.

■ Choose and read a book provided by your teacher and think about the sequence of events. Write a short paragraph that uses signal words to tell the sequence.

W9-ARV-797

Read for Meaning

Generalize

15 min.

You will need
- Leveled Readers
- paper
- pencils

● Read the book you chose from those provided by your teacher. Think about how the characters behave. Write one sentence stating a generalization about a character. Write one sentence with a detail that supports your generalization.

▲ Read the book you chose from those provided by your teacher and make a generalization about a character's behavior. Write one sentence stating your generalization. Write two sentences with story details that support your generalization.

■ As you read the book you chose from those provided by your teacher, make a generalization about a character. Write a short paragraph stating your generalization. Include at least three details from the story that support your generalization.

Read for Meaning

Sequence

15 min.

You will need

- Leveled Readers
- paper
- pencil

● Choose and read a book provided by your teacher. Think about the sequence of events in the story. Write sentences telling three events in the story. Use signal words, such as *first, next,* and *finally* to show the sequence.

▲ Choose and read a book provided by your teacher and think about the sequence of events in the story. Write three sentences that tell the sequence. Use signal words, such as *first, next, then,* and *finally* to show sequence.

■ As you read a book provided by your teacher, think about the story's sequence of events. Write a short paragraph telling the sequence of at least four important story events. Use signal words.

Read for Meaning

Sequence

15 min.

You will need

- Leveled Readers
- paper
- pencils

● Read the book you chose from those provided by your teacher. Think about the order of events in the story. Write three sentences telling the sequence of events. Use signal words, such as *first, next,* and *finally* to show the sequence.

▲ Read the book you chose from those provided by your teacher and think about the story's sequence of events. Write a short paragraph that tells the sequence of events. Use signal words, such as *first, next, then,* and *finally*.

■ As you read a book your chose from those provided by your teacher, think about the story's sequence of events. Write a paragraph that tells the story's most important events. Use signal words to help show the sequence.

Read for Meaning

Author's Purpose

15 min.

You will need
- Leveled Readers
- paper
- pencil

● Choose and read a book provided by your teacher. Think about the author's purpose for writing the story. Write one sentence that tells the author's purpose.

▲ Choose and read a book provided by your teacher and think about the author's purpose for writing the story. Write one sentence stating the author's purpose. Explain whether you think the purpose was achieved.

■ As you read a book provided by your teacher, think about the author's reason for writing. Write a short paragraph stating the author's purpose and whether you think the purpose was achieved.

Read for Meaning

Fact and Opinion

15 min.

You will need
- Leveled Readers
- paper
- pencils

● Read the book you chose from those provided by your teacher. Think about the information and ideas the author includes. Write one sentence that states a fact from the selection. Write one sentence that states an opinion.

▲ Read the book you chose from those provided by your teacher and think about the facts and opinions the author includes. Write two sentences that give facts from the selection. Write two sentences that give the author's opinion.

■ As you read the book you chose from those provided by your teacher, distinguish between statements of fact and statements of opinion. Write a short paragraph stating facts from the selection. Write a short paragraph giving examples of opinions.

Read for Meaning

Plot, Character, and Setting

15 min.

You will need

- Leveled Readers
- paper
- pencil

● Choose a book from those your teacher provided. Write one sentence telling about a character. Write one sentence telling the setting of the story. Then explain the story's plot.

▲ Read one of the books your teacher provided and think about the characters, setting, and the plot. Write a short paragraph describing each of these.

■ Read one of the books your teacher provided. Think about the literary elements of character, setting, and plot. Write a paragraph that discusses these elements. Include details from the story in your paragraph.

Read for Meaning

Cause and Effect

15 min.

You will need
- Leveled Readers
- paper
- pencils

● Read and choose a book provided by your teacher. Think about causes and effects in the selection. Write one sentence stating a cause. Write one sentence explaining the effect.

▲ Read and choose a book provided by your teacher and think about the causes and effects in the selection. Write a short paragraph detailing a cause in the selection. Include sentences explaining the effects of the cause.

■ As you read a book your chose from the books your teacher provided think about the causes and effects in the selection. Write a paragraph detailing a cause from the selection. Include details explaining the effects of this cause.

Author's Purpose

You will need

15 min.

- Leveled Readers
- paper
- pencil

● Choose and read one of the books your teacher provided. Think about the author's purpose for writing. Write a short paragraph that tells what the author's purpose is.

▲ Choose and read one of the books your teacher provided. Write a short paragraph that explains the author's purpose and whether you think he or she achieved the purpose.

■ Choose and read one of the books your teacher provided. Write a paragraph stating the author's purpose and whether the author achieved the purpose.

Draw Conclusions

You will need

15 min.

- Leveled Readers
- paper
- pencils

● Read a book provided by your teacher. What conclusion can you draw about the main character? Write one sentence stating your conclusion. Write one sentence with a story detail that supports your conclusion.

▲ Read a book provided by your teacher. Draw a conclusion about the main character. Write one sentence stating your conclusion. Write two sentences with story details that support your conclusion.

■ Read a book provided by your teacher and draw a conclusion about the story's main character. Write a short paragraph that states your conclusion. Include sentences with story details that support your conclusion.

Read for Meaning

Main Idea and Details

15 min.

You will need
- Leveled Readers
- pencil
- paper

● Choose and read a leveled reader provided by your teacher. Think about the main idea. Write one sentence that tells the selection's main idea and one sentence with a detail that tells more this idea.

▲ Choose and read a leveled reader provided by your teacher. Think about the main idea. Write one sentence stating the main idea. Write two sentences with supporting details.

■ Choose and read a leveled reader provided by your teacher. Think about the selection's main idea. Write a short paragraph that states the main idea and supporting details.

Read for Meaning

Main Idea and Details

15 min.

You will need
- Leveled Readers
- paper
- pencils

● Read one of the books your teacher provides. Think about what the selection is mostly about. Write one sentence stating the main idea of the selection. Write one sentence with a detail that supports your opinion.

▲ Read one of the books your teacher provides and think about what it is mostly about. Write one sentence stating the selection's main idea. Write two sentences with details that support your opinion.

■ As you read a book provided by your teacher, think about the selection's main idea. Write a short paragraph that states the book's main idea. Include sentences with story details that help support your opinion.

Read for Meaning

Cause and Effect

15 min.

You will need
- Leveled Readers
- paper
- pencil

● Choose and read a leveled reader provided by your teacher. Think about what happens in the story and what causes it to happen. Write one sentence that tells an effect. Write one sentence explaining the cause of effect.

▲ Choose and read a leveled reader provided by your teacher. Think about what happens in the story. Write sentences that give examples of two causes and two effects from the story. Note any effects that have more than one cause.

■ Choose and read a leveled reader provided by your teacher. Think about the causes and effects in the story. Give three examples of cause and effect from the story. Write your examples in complete sentences.

Read for Meaning

Character, Plot, and Theme

15 min.

You will need
- Leveled Readers
- paper
- pencils

● Choose and read one of the books your teacher provides. Write one sentence telling who the characters are in the story. Write one sentence explaining the story's plot. Finally, write one sentence stating the theme of the story.

▲ Choose and read one of the books your teacher provides. Write a short paragraph about the story. Include information about the story's characters. Describe the story's plot and explain the theme of the story.

■ Choose and read one of the books your teacher provides and write a paragraph telling about the literary elements of character, plot, and theme. Include story details that support your opinion about the theme of the story.

Read for Meaning

Draw Conclusions

15 min.

You will need
- Leveled Readers
- paper
- pencils

● Choose and read a leveled reader provided by your teacher. Think of a conclusion you can draw based on information in the story. Write one sentence stating a conclusion. Write one sentence with a story detail that supports your conclusion.

▲ Choose and read a leveled reader provided by your teacher. Think about conclusions you can draw based on textual evidence. Write sentences stating two conclusions. Support each conclusion with a detail from the story.

■ Choose and read a leveled reader provided by your teacher. Think about conclusions you can draw based on textual evidence. Write a paragraph stating your conclusions. Include details from the story that support each of your conclusions.

 Grade 4, Unit 2, Week 3

Read for Meaning

Compare and Contrast

15 min.

You will need
- Leveled Readers
- paper
- pencils

● Choose and read one of the books your teacher provides. How does the setting of the selection compare to the setting in another story you have read? Write one sentence comparing the settings. Write one sentence contrasting them.

▲ Choose and read one of the books your teacher provides. Think about how the setting compares to the setting in another story you have read. Write two sentences comparing the settings. Write two sentences contrasting them.

■ Choose and read one of the books your teacher provides. Compare and contrast the setting of the selection to the setting in another story you have read. Write a short paragraph comparing the settings. Write a short paragraph contrasting the settings.

Read for Meaning

Draw Conclusions

15 min.

You will need
- Leveled Readers
- paper
- pencils

● Choose a book from those your teacher provided. Think of a conclusion you can draw based on information in the book. Write one sentence stating a conclusion. Write one sentence with a detail that supports your conclusion.

▲ Read one of the books your teacher provided and think about conclusions you can draw based on evidence in the book. Write sentences stating two conclusions. Support each conclusion with a detail.

■ Choose and read a leveled reader. Think about conclusions you can draw based on evidence in the book. Write a paragraph stating your conclusions. Include details that support each conclusion.

Read for Meaning

Author's Purpose

15 min.

You will need
- Leveled Readers
- paper
- pencils

● Choose and read one of the books your teacher provides. Think about the author's purpose for writing the selection. Write a sentence stating the author's purpose. Write a sentence with a detail from the selection that supports your opinion.

▲ Choose and read one of the books your teacher provides, and think about the author's purpose. Write one sentence stating the author's purpose. Write two sentences with details from the selection that support your opinion.

■ As you read a book provided by your teacher, think about the author's purpose for writing. Write a short paragraph stating the author's purpose. Include three details from the selection that support your opinion.

Read for Meaning

Fact and Opinion

15 min.

You will need
- Leveled Readers
- paper
- pencils

● Choose and read a book provided by your teacher. Think about the information and ideas the author provides. Write one sentence stating a fact from the selection. Write one sentence that states an opinion.

▲ Choose and read a book provided by your teacher. Think about the facts and opinions the author presents. Write two statements of fact from the selection. Write two statements of opinion.

■ As you read a book you chose from those provided by your teacher, think about the facts and opinions the author presents. Write a short paragraph giving statements of fact from the selection. Write a short paragraph with examples of statements of opinion.

Read for Meaning

Character and Plot

15 min.

You will need
- Leveled Readers
- paper
- pencils

● Choose and read one of the books your teacher provides. Write one sentence describing a character in the story. Think about the story events. Write a sentence that explains the story's plot.

▲ Choose and read one of the books your teacher provides and think about the events that happen in the story. Write a sentence that tells the story's plot. Then write sentences that describe two of the characters in the story.

■ As you read the book you chose, think about the plot of the story and its characters. Write two short paragraphs explaining the story's plot and characters.

Read for Meaning

Main Idea and Details

You will need

- Leveled Readers
- paper
- pencils

15 min.

● Choose and read a book from those your teacher provided. Think about the selection's main idea. Write one sentence stating the main idea. Write one sentence with a detail telling more about the main idea.

▲ Choose and read a book from those your teacher provided. Think about the selection's main idea. Write one sentence stating the main idea. Write two details that give more information about this idea.

■ Choose a book from those your teacher provided. As you read, think about the book's main idea and the details that support it. Write a paragraph telling the selection's main idea. Include three details that tell more about this main idea.

Graphic Sources

15 min.

You will need
- Leveled Readers
- paper
- pencils

● Choose and read a book provided by your teacher. Study the information in the graphic sources. Write a sentence telling what graphic sources are in the book. Choose one. Tell what facts it provides.

▲ Choose and read a book provided by your teacher. Study the graphic sources. Write a sentence that names the different graphic sources in your book. Choose two and explain what information they provide.

■ Choose a book provided by your teacher. As you read, notice the information presented in the graphic sources. Write a short paragraph describing the different graphic sources. Give details about the information each one provides.

Read for Meaning

Graphic Sources

15 min.

You will need
- Leveled Readers
- paper
- pencils

● Choose and read a book provided by your teacher. Pay attention the information presented in the graphic sources. Choose one graphic source. Write one sentence telling about the information the graphic source provides.

▲ Choose and read a book provided by your teacher. Notice the graphic sources. Write one sentence stating the different graphic sources in your book. Choose one and describe the information it provides.

■ Choose and read a book provided by your teacher. Notice the different graphic sources. Write a short paragraph that describes the different types of graphic sources in the book and explains the information they provide.

Read for Meaning

Sequence

15 min.

You will need
- Leveled Readers
- paper
- pencils

● Choose and read a book provided by your teacher. Think about the order of events in the selection. Write three sentences telling the sequence of events. Use signal words, such as *first, next,* and *finally* to show the sequence.

▲ Choose and read a book provided by your teacher. Think about the selection's sequence of events. Write four sentences that tell the sequence of events. Use signal words, such as *first, next, then,* and *finally.*

■ Chose a book provided by your teacher. As you read, think about the selection's sequence of events. Write a short paragraph that tells the selection's most important events. Use signal words to help show the sequence.

Read for Meaning

Fact and Opinion

15 min.

You will need
- Leveled Readers
- paper
- pencils

● Choose and read a book provided by your teacher. Think about the facts and opinions the author expresses. Write one sentence stating a fact from the selection. Write one sentence that includes the author's opinion.

▲ Choose a book provided by your teacher. After reading it, find two statements of fact the author expresses and two statements of opinion. Write your findings in complete sentences.

■ Choose a book provided by your teacher. After reading it, write a short paragraph with three statements of fact the author provides. Next write a short paragraph stating three opinions the author gives.

Read for Meaning

Compare and Contrast

You will need

15 min.

- Leveled Readers
- paper
- pencils

● Choose and read a book provided by your teacher. How does the setting in the selection compare and contrast to where you live? Write one sentence that compares the settings. Write one sentence that contrasts them.

▲ Choose and read a book provided by your teacher. Think about how the setting of the selection compares and contrasts to where you live. Write two sentences comparing the places. Write two sentences contrasting them.

■ Choose a book provided by your teacher. As you read, think about comparisons and contrasts between your city and the selection's setting. Write a short paragraph comparing the locations. Write a short paragraph contrasting them.

Read for Meaning

Generalize

15 min.

You will need
- Leveled Readers
- paper
- pencils

● Choose and read a book provided by your teacher. Think about a generalization you can make. Write one sentence stating your generalization. Write one sentence with a story detail that supports your generalization.

▲ Choose and read a book provided by your teacher. Make a generalization based on information in the story. Write one sentence stating the generalization. Write two sentences with story details that support your generalization.

■ Choose a book provided by your teacher. As you read it, think about generalizations you can make. Write a short paragraph stating your generalizations. For each generalization, include a story detail that supports your opinion.

Read for Meaning

Compare and Contrast

You will need

- Leveled Readers
- paper
- pencils

15 min.

● Choose and read a book provided by your teacher. Think about how two characters in the story are alike and different. Write one sentence that compares the characters. Write one sentence that contrasts the characters.

▲ Choose and read a book provided by your teacher. Think about comparisons and contrasts between two characters. Write two sentences comparing the characters. Write two sentences contrasting the characters.

■ Choose a book provided by your teacher. As you read it, compare and contrast two story characters. Write a short paragraph that compares the characters. Write another short paragraph that contrasts the characters.

Read for Meaning

Cause and Effect

15 min.

You will need

- Leveled Readers
- paper
- pencils

● Choose and read a book provided by your teacher. Think about something that happens. Write one sentence that tells about an effect. Write one sentence that tells the cause of this effect.

▲ Choose and read a book provided by your teacher. Think about what happens. Write about two effects that happen in the selection. For each effect, write a sentence stating the cause.

■ Choose a book provided by your teacher. As you read, think about the causes and effects in the selection. Write a short paragraph describing three causes and three effects. Note the most important cause-and-effect relationship.

Generalize

15 min.

You will need
- Leveled Readers
- paper
- pencils

● Read a book provided by your teacher. Make a generalization about the story's main character. Write a sentence with a story detail that supports it.

▲ Read a book provided by your teacher. Make a generalization about the story's main character. Write a sentence stating your generalization. Write two sentences with story details that support your generalization.

■ Read a book provided by your teacher and make a generalization about a character in the story. Write a short paragraph that states your generalization and include details from the story that support your generalization.